THE HUNGARIAN CUISINE

The aim of life is nothing but eating and drinking well – says the Hungarian protagonist of a well-known operetta. We do not say that this is a typical Hungarian philosophy but it is obviously true that a typical Hungarian meal is a row of plentiful, delicious dishes containing a lot of calories. To warm up before getting started, let's drink a glass of good Hungarian plum or apricot brandy.

What shall we prepare for? Sautéed onion, sweet paprika, the indispensable component of Hungarian cuisine – sour cream, strong spices and the dominance of pork, beef and poultry dishes. All the travelers who have visited Hungary at least once must surely remember the piquant aroma of Goulash Soup and Veal Ragout with Red Wine. It is no wonder that the trinity of lard-onion-sweet paprika comes to mind when we hear the expression "Hungarian Cuisine" – Goulash Soup and Stew are both based on these ingredients. This is an interesting feature of Hungarian Gastronomy. Originally Goulash and Stew were the Hungarian shepherds' simple food and the usage of sweet paprika became widespread here only in the 1700s.

But where did Hungarian Cuisine start off? If the first Hungarian cookbook had been made 1000 years earlier, during the time of the conquest, we could read about ground cereals cooked in water or milk, about marinated meat and soured horse milk. If we went back to the 15th century we would please the gourmet reader with fantastic recipes. Naturally, it is a lady we should thank for this daring diversity. The second wife of King Matthias, the most popular king of the Hungarians, Beatrice from Naples, added a bit of Italian flavor to the excellent ingredients of the Hungarian motherland. The aristocrats' tables were flooded with roasts served in sauces – beef, veal, lamb, pork, goat, deer, venison, hare, goose, duck, partridge, pheasant, turkey and fat peacock were served with cinnamon, black pepper, ginger, anise and chestnut. The first leavened breads were baked in traditional ovens; the inner parts of these breads were used to thicken different soups and sauces. The Italians brought their delicious cheese and cooked pastas and with Hungarian cottage cheese the first cottage cheese pasta was ready – served with sour cream and fried bacon cubes it is a fantastic dish!

It is thanks to the Ottoman occupation in the 16th-17th century (and not a lady this time) that eastern aromas and base materials were added to Hungarian Cuisine. However it came into being, it is gratitude we should feel for being able to enjoy tasty cabbage rolls, scones, or sweets filled with poppy seed or walnut, drinking coffee towards the pashas and their subjects. What's more, we should thank them for the sweet paprika as well, as it appeared in Hungary at that time.

Gourmets should pay their gratitude to the neighboring Austrians, too with whom – besides being geographically close – we shared a long stretch of our history. They taught Hungarian chefs how to make a special thickening (flour sautéed on oil) which is a basic element of preparing many different vegetable side dishes and without which we cannot imagine a delicious coated meat, cottage cheese strudel or plum dumpling.

If your mouth is watering by now, it is high time to purchase a big portion of sweet paprika, take this little cookbook and start cooking! And while working, do not forget what the author of a cookbook from 1604 advises: ... First and foremost, the chef should be in a very good mood!

STARTERS

Cold Larded Venison Saddle

Ingredients:

800 gr/28 oz venison saddle
1 tablespoon mustard
ground black pepper, salt
oil
120 gr/4 oz smoked bacon
600 gr/21 oz thick French salad
lettuce leaves

fresh or dried fruit

Preparation:

1. Remove the meat from the bone on both sides. Remove the thin skin, and rub with mustard and black pepper. Lay in a pot and pour oil on top to cover. Cover and marinate in the refrigerator for 2-3 days, turn from time to time.

2. Put some salt and a few drops of vinegar in the water, and cook the bone until all the meat comes off.

3. Cut the smoked bacon into 0.5 cm/0.25" strips and add to the marinated meat. Add some salt and tie with strips.

4. Pour 7 tablespoons of the oil used for marinating into the pan, heat it, and fry the meat. Place the meat into a casserole, pour the hot oil on top, and then put it into a pre-heated oven (200°C/390F; 180°C/350F, in air-convector ovens). Roast it rare, medium or well-done.

5. For rare venison roast for 15 minutes. The meat should be done only on the outside, the inside is pink, and the middle is raw. The medium venison requires 20 minutes in the oven and not only the skin is done but the inside as well, 1 cm/0.2" deep, the middle is pink but no blood in it. The well-done version requires 6 more minutes.

6. Cool down when ready, and then put it into the refrigerator to congeal a bit. Remove the strings, and slice the meat into 3-4 mm thick pieces.

7. Place the bone on a serving plate. Lay French salad along the two sides then place the meat on the salad. Decorate with lettuce leaves and fruit.

Meat Crepes as in Hortobágy

Ingredients:

650 gr/23 oz veal shoulder or veal leg
1 onion, 2 cloves of garlic
4 tablespoons oil
1 tablespoon sweet paprika
1 green pepper and tomato each
1/2 teaspoon ground caraway seeds
1 teaspoon salt
1/2 teaspoon red hot pepper paste
1.5 dl/5 oz sour cream
1 tablespoon flour
12 crepes without sugar
20 gr/0.7 oz butter

Preparation:

1. Cut the meat into 2 cm/0.8" cubes. Chop the onion finely. Sauté the onion, add the meat cubes and cook them stirring until the meat cubes turn white.

2. Remove from the hotplate and add the sweet paprika. Add the chopped green pepper and tomato, and then the crushed garlic, caraway seeds, salt and pepper paste. Pour a bit of water (app. 1.5 dl/5 oz) under it and steam, under cover, for about 1.5 hours until tender. Replace the evaporated water by small amounts when necessary making sure the water never fully covers the meat so it does not cook instead of steaming. When done it should have a thick sauce.

3. Mix the sour cream and the flour with 1.5 dl/5 oz cold water (or cream) until smooth, add to the stew then boil for 2-3 minutes, stirring continuously. If too thick, add some water (cream) to it.

4. Strain the stew, then cut the veal into small pieces (mince it when preparing bigger quantity). In order to avoid drying, mix with 1-2 teaspoons stew sauce.

5. Heap one spoonful of filling into the middle of each crepe, fold into quarters and then line them up in a buttered casserole.

6. Strain the sauce, pour on the crepes and put into the oven for a short time just to warm. Make sure not to burn.

3

Cold Goose Liver with Onion

Ingredients:

650 gr/23 oz goose bacon
500 gr/18 oz fat goose liver
1/2 teaspoon salt
a few pieces of whole black pepper
1 bay leaf
1 small and 2 big onions
1 small apple, 1 egg
1-2 cloves of garlic
2-3 tablespoons flour
1/2 teaspoon sweet paprika
3 tablespoons breadcrumbs
oil

Preparation:

1. Cut the goose bacon into 2 cm/0.8" cubes and fry it stirring from time to time. Pull aside and remove the cracklings.

2. Put the liver in the fat after cooling (if too hot, it might burn the liver), add some salt, pepper and a bay leaf, as well as the peeled garlic, the onion and apple washed and cut into halves without peeling.

3. As the oil heats up again, reduce the heat, fry the liver for 18-20 minutes, and then let it cool in its own fat. Using a skimmer put the liver carefully in a small pot, and strain the fat over it. It should cover the liver completely.

4. Peel the onion, cut it into 0.5 cm/0.2" slices, and separate the rings. To make the coating, dip the rings first into flour, then into beaten eggs, and then into breadcrumbs flavored with sweet paprika. Fry them in oil for about 2 minutes. Place them on paper towel to soak the excess oil.

5. With a knife dipped into hot water cut not too thick slices. Serve with hot crispy onion rings and toasted bread.

Pork in Aspic

Ingredients:

4 pork knuckles (app. 1.7 kg/3.75 lb)
1 pork leg (app. 1.2 kg/2.65 lb)
800 gr/28 oz pork head with its skin on
400 gr/14 oz pork rind
600 gr/21 oz pork shoulder
6-8 parsnips (max. 800 gr/28 oz)
3-4 carrots
12 cloves of garlic
2 onions
2-3 tablespoons salt or spice mixture
30-35 pieces of whole black pepper
1/2 bunch of parsley and celery leaves each
2-3 boiled eggs
parsley
ground black pepper, sweet paprika

Preparation:

1. Clean all the meat. Split the knuckles along-side, cut the back knuckles into 3 pieces.
2. Clean the parsnips, carrots and garlic and wash onions in their skin. Place the vegetables and meat into a big pot, add about 5 1/5 quart water, add some salt, whole black peppers, parsley and celery leave. Cook over high heat, and then cover with a lid leaving a small gap for the steam.
3. Cook for app. 2.5 hours on low heat without stirring. Let it settle for 15 minutes, and then carefully strain it through a piece of clean cloth or gauze. Make sure the liquid stays clean and transparent.
4. Let the meat and carrots cool down, cover and put into the refrigerator. Put the liquid in a cold place for the whole night. Next day remove the fat.
5. Remove the bones from the soft leg and head, slice the meat into pieces and distribute them into 4 bowls. Place the cut and de-boned knuckles, a piece of rind and 1-2 slices of shoulder into each dish. Decorate them with nicely cut hard-boiled eggs, carrot rings and parsley. Warm the aspic until it melts and ladle into the dishes. Let stand in a cold place until the liquid hardens.
6. When serving, place the bowls in hot water fora few seconds then turn out contents on plate. Decorate with ground pepper and sweet paprika. Serve with pickles, horseradish in vinegar and fresh bread.

Hungarian Fish Soup

Ingredients:

a small carp (app. 1.2 kg/2.5 lb)
1 tablespoon sweet pepper
1-2 hot peppers
(or 1 teaspoon hot paprika cream)
salt
3 onions

Preparation:

1. Clean the carp, put the milt and spawns aside, cut the head off. Fillet the body and remove the skin. Slit the fillets deeply every 2-3 mm/0.1" and cut them into medium-size slices or 2.5 cm/1" cubes. Rub them thoroughly with a teaspoon of salt, sweet paprika and hot paprika cream – the hot peppers should be put into the soup. Cover and put into the refrigerator for 1 hour.

2. Clean the onions, slice into thin rings, and place into a pot or stewpot containing app. 2 1/2 quart of water. Add the bones and the cleaned head and boil with a tablespoon of salt. Cover with a lid leaving a small gap for the steam and cook for 1.5 hours. If desired, you can add a bunch of parsley, 1 tomato or green pepper.

3. Remove from the heat, strain and using a wooden spoon crush the onion through a sieve into the strained broth. Remove the meat from the bones and the head and crush it.

4. Boil the thick broth, add the marinated fish cubes or slices and the roe, and cook for 6-8 minutes. Add some salt if needed and taste it with some extra hot peppers.

Goose Soup with Liver Dumplings

Ingredients:

3 goose wings, goose necks, goose backs each
3 carrots and parsnips each
1 kohlrabi and celery each
1 bunch of parsley, 1-2 celery leaves
2 cloves of garlic, 1.5 onions
1 teaspoon whole black pepper
hot paprika cream, salt, 1 marjoram
300 gr/10.6 oz goose liver
2 rolls, 2 eggs
2 tablespoons flour
6 tablespoons breadcrumbs
1/2 teaspoon ground black pepper
2 tablespoons oil

Preparation:

1. Wash the goose giblets, remove the skin. Cut the wings and gizzards into halves, the necks into smaller pieces. Place them in a pot, pour 5 1/5 quart water on the top, boil it and then strain the foam. Clean the vegetables. Cut the carrots into quarters, the kohlrabi and celery into halves and drop all along with the parsley and celery leaves into the soup. Add the cleaned garlic. Wash the onion; add it to the soup without peeling. Taste it, and cook on low heat for 2 hours, put aside for a short time then strain.

2. Liver dumplings: soak the rolls in water, squeeze and mince it together with the liver. Mix it with the eggs and the flour, and then spice with salt, marjoram and black pepper. Chop the parsley and the cleaned and peeled onion finely, sauté then add to the liver. Let stand for 10 minutes.

3. Wet your hands and form 8 big dumplings from the paste. Cook them in salty boiling water. It is practical to cook only one first to see whether it is too soft. In case it is, you can add some more flour.

4. Strain the soup before serving, place 1 big dumpling in each plate, and then ladle the hot soup on it. Serve the nicely chopped soft vegetables and giblets in a big plate, separately.

Tarragon Game Ragout

Ingredients:

400 gr/14 oz de-
boned haunch or
shoulder (or legs)
of venison
1 onion, 2 carrots
4 tablespoons oil
1 bay leaf
1 teasp. salt
1 parsnip
200 gr/7 oz small
champignons
150 gr/5.3 oz
green peas
1 bouillon cube or
1 teasp. spice mix-
ture
1 teasp. mustard
juice of 1/2 lemon
dash of ground
black pepper
1/2 teasp. marjo-
ram
1 dl/3.4 oz sour
cream
1 dl/3.4 oz whole
cream
1 tablespoon flour
1 bunch of fresh
or 1 teasp. dried
tarragon leaves

Preparation:

1. Wash and dry the meat, remove the ligaments and foils, and cut into 1 cm/0.5" cubes.
2. Chop the cleaned onion finely; heat the oil, sauté the meat with the onion on medium heat for 4-5 minutes until the meat turns white. Add the bay leaf, some salt and a bit of water, then steam, covered, for 50 minutes until tender. Take off the lid and continue cooking until the water evaporates.
3. Clean the vegetables. Cut carrots and parsnip into 1 cm/0.5" cubes or half-rings, the mushroom into wedges. Mix the vegetables with the meat and cook for about 3-4 minutes. Add app

1.2 l/1.2 quart water, green peas and the bouillon cube crushed. Boil, and then cook for 20 minutes until everything is tender. Mix the mustard with lemon juice, black pepper, marjoram and a bit of water and pour it into the soup.
4. Mix the cream and sour cream with the flour until smooth. Ladle a bit of hot soup on it. Pour the mixture into the soup and cook for 2-3 minutes to let it thicken.
5. Wash the tarragon; pick the leaves off the stem, chop finely. Put in the soup, and boil for 1-2 minutes to preserve the characteristic flavor.
6. Remove the inner part of some small loaves and ladle the soup in them to serve.

Cold Sour Cherry Soup

Ingredients:

small piece of whole cinnamon
(or 1/2 teaspoon ground cinnamon)
3-4 cloves, 1 tablespoon flour
1 1/34 oz water
500 gr/18 oz sour cherry, pits removed (frozen or preserved)
3-4 tablespoons sugar, dash of salt

juice of 1/2 lemon
1 dl/3.4 oz sour cream and cream each

Preparation:

1. Put the cinnamon and the cloves in the water and cook for 4-5 minutes. Add the sour cherry, sweeten it with sugar, add some salt, lemon juice and cook until tender.
2. Mix the cream and sour cream with the flour until smooth. Ladle a bit of hot soup on it then add to the soup to thicken it. Serve cold.

Bean Soup with Pork Knuckle and Cabbage

Ingredients:

250 gr/9 oz dried beans
450 gr/16 oz de-boned smoked meat
2 bay leaves
1 teaspoon whole black pepper
3-4 cloves of garlic
500 gr/18 oz sour cabbage/sourkraut
1 big onion
5-6 tablespoons oil
1 tablespoon sweet paprika
1 green pepper
1 tomato
3 dl/10 oz sour cream
1 tablespoon flour
salt, ground hot paprika

Preparation:

1. Soak the beans overnight in cold water. Strain the following day and cook. Reduce heat when starts boiling and cook almost until tender.
2. Place the smoked meat in water with the bay leaves, whole peppers and garlic and cook until tender. Let it cool down in its own liquid.
3. If the sourkraut is too sour let soak in cold water a few minutes then drain. Chop if stripes too long. Clean the onion, chop finely, put in a medium size pot, and sauté. Add the sweet paprika, mix and pour a bit of water on it. Add sourkraut then the finely chopped tomato and green pepper to taste. Cook covered on medium heat until crispy and add the strained, almost tender beans. Add the water used to cook the meat, cover and cook over low heat until tender.
4. Chop the smoked meat into 2-3 cm/1" cubes and add to the beans and cabbage. Mix the sour cream and flour until smooth. Ladle a bit of hot soup on it, then add the mixture to the soup and cook for a few minutes to let it thicken. Add hot paprika to taste.

2 tablespoons sweet paprika
salt
2 green peppers
2 tomatoes
1 teaspoon hot paprika pasta
5 carrots
3 parsnips, 1 egg
2 kg/4.4 lb potatoes
100 gr/3.5 oz flour home made dumplings

Preparation:

1. Chop the beef leg into 2 cm/1" cubes. Sauté the onion on medium heat, add the meat and stir until the meat turns white.

2. Chop the garlic and caraway seeds finely, add them to the meat. Add sweet paprika. Mix, and pour 2 dl/6.7 oz water on it. Add the salt and the finely chopped green pepper and tomato to taste. Spice with the paprika cream and cook on medium heat, covered, for about 1.5 hours until almost tender.

3. Chop the carrots and parsnips into rings, add them to the meat and steam together while cleaning the potatoes and chopping them into 2.5 cm/1" cubes. Add the potatoes to the meat and pour as much water to it as much soup we want to make (app. 3.5 l/3.6 quart), then cook. Place some green pepper and tomato cut in halves in the soup. Cook covered for 15 minutes, add the dumplings then cook for another 15 minutes until done. Add more salt or spices to taste.

Goulash Soup

Ingredients:

1.5 kg/3.3 lb de-boned beef leg
2 onions
7 tablespoons oil or 100 gr/3.5 oz cooking lard
4 cloves of garlic
1/2 teaspoon caraway seeds

Potatoes as Side Dish with Fried Sausage

Ingredients:

1.5 kg/3.3 lb potato
1/2 tablespoon salt, 1 tablespoon flour
2 bay leaves
2 dl/6.7 oz sour cream
1/2 teaspoon sweet paprika
4 sausages
2-3 tablespoons oil
1 teaspoon 10% vinegar

Preparation:

1. Peel the potatoes and chop them into 0.5 cm/0.2" thick rings. Place them into a pot, pour about 7-8 dl/27 oz water on it and add salt. Add the bay leaves, boil over high heat, and then cook for 15 minutes over low heat, covered, until tender.
2. Mix the sour cream with the flour until smooth, add a ladleful of the hot cooking water, add the sweet paprika, stir well, pour the mixture into the pot and boil for 2 minutes. Spice with few drops of vinegar. Serve with fried sausage or a piece of fried meat, but it is also delicious on its own, without any toppings.
3. Cut in the top of the sausages on both sides (if you cut in small crosses, the sausage opens up nicely when fried). Put some oil in a pan and fry the sausage in the oil for 3-4 minutes until it turns a bit red.
4. Add the oil used for frying to the dish; it adds a wonderful flavor.

Cornmeal with Mushrooms and Sour Cream

Ingredients:

400 gr/14 oz champignons
1 small onion
1 l/34 oz water
(or milk)
salt
ground black pepper
1 small bunch of parsley
250 gr/8.8 oz corn-grits
50 gr/1.8 oz butter
3 dl/10 oz sour cream
100 gr mild cheese
3 tablespoons oil

Preparation:

1. Clean the champignons and chop them into pieces. Peel and chop the onion finely, sauté stirring continuously. Add the champignons and sauté for a few minutes stirring occasionally. Add salt, black pepper and finely chopped parsley.

2. Boil the water (milk), pour the corn-grits while stirring and add a bit of salt.

3. Cook for 4-5 minutes, stirring until the sauce thickens. Pull aside, and then put a lid on for 10 minutes so that the grids can get completely soft in the steam.

3. Butter the inside of a casserole, and using a tablespoon dipped in melted oil "chop" the cornmeal into it. Pile the sautéed mushrooms on, pour on the sour cream and grate the cheese on top.

4. Bake in a preheated oven, over medium heat (200°C/390F; 180°C/350F in air-convector ovens) for 7-8 minutes until the cheese melts nicely.

Layered Potatoes

Ingredients:

6 potatoes (1.2 kg/2.6 lb)
salt, ground black pepper
4.5 dl/15 oz sour cream
6 hard-boiled eggs
250-300 gr/9-10 oz sausage

for buttering the casserole:

butter, or baking margarine
breadcrumbs
100 gr mild cheese

Preparation:

1. Scrub the potatoes with a brush, cook with their skin on in slightly salty water until soft. It is done when you can easily pierce with a needle.

2. Drain, let cool a bit, peel and chop into 0.5 cm/0.2" slices. Butter the inside of a medium size (20 x 30 cm – 8x14") casserole or small baking dish, coat with breadcrumbs and lay half of the potatoes at the bottom. Add some salt, black pepper and spread half of the sour cream on it.

3. Slice the eggs and the cleaned sausage into nice rings and arrange them evenly on the potatoes. Cover with the remaining potatoes, add some salt, black pepper and spread the remaining half of the sour cream on it. Grate some cheese on top, and then bake it over high heat (200°C/390F; 180°C/350F in air-convector ovens) for 15-20 minutes.

4. For vegetarians you can substitute the sausage with sautéed mushrooms. To create a very special dish, instead of sausage you can add some canned sardines or tuna fish in oil.

Stuffed Cabbage

Ingredients:

200 gr/7 oz rice
150 gr/5.3 oz smoked bacon
2 tablespoons oil
1 big onion
4 cloves of garlic
600 gr/21 oz ground thin flank
1 tablespoon sweet paprika
1/2 teaspoon ground caraway seeds
salt
ground black pepper
1 teaspoon marjoram
1 bunch of dill
12 medium size pickled cabbage leaves
1.4-1.6 kg/3.5 lb pickled cabbage
1 teaspoon hot paprika cream
2 x 1.5 dl/5 oz sour cream
1 egg

Preparation:

1. Boil 2 dl/6.7 oz water. Add the rice and some salt and cook, covered, until half-done. Chop the bacon into small cubes and fry it over 2 tablespoons of oil. Peel and chop the onion finely, add it to the bacon and sauté. Pull aside, and add a third of it to the rice.

2. Add the ground pork, the egg and sweet paprika, ground garlic, half of the caraway seeds, black pepper, marjoram and salt, then mix well. Fill the cabbage leaves with the mixture and form meatballs from the rest.

3. Shorten the small cabbage stripes a bit. Sprinkle the onion and bacon left in the pan with sweet paprika, heat stirring and add 1 dl/3.4 oz water. Add the cabbage slices, caraway seeds, ground garlic and paprika paste. Arrange the filling on the top. Boil over high heat, cover and cook over low heat for 1.5 hours until tender.

4. When done, finely chop the dill, mix with the sour cream, add to the cabbage, boil for a few minutes and if needed, add some salt and spices.

Pepper and Tomato Stew

Ingredients:

600 gr/21 oz tomato
2 big onions
1.5 kg/3.3 lb green pepper
200 gr/7 oz bacon
3 tablespoons oil
1 tablespoon sweet paprika
1.5 teaspoons salt
1/2 teaspoon hot paprika paste
1 teaspoon sweet paprika paste
200 gr/7 oz sausage

Preparation:

1. Wash the tomatoes, remove the stems, and chop them into quarters or medium size cubes. Remove the stems of the green peppers, and chop them into big cubes. Chop the peeled and cleaned onions finely.

2. Chop the bacon into small cubes and sauté in a pot. Add the onion and sauté it, stirring, for a few minutes until turns gold. Pull aside and add the sweet paprika.

3. Add the tomato immediately to prevent the paprika from burning. Add a bit of salt, and then cook over low heat for app. 10 minutes. If the tomato is not juicy enough, add some water. It is done when the tomato and the onion make a thick paste. Add half of the green pepper, the two different types of paprika paste and cook, over low heat, for 15 minutes until tender. Stir a few times and add some sausage rings too.

4. Let it cool a bit, mince and cook it again. Add the remaining pepper and sausages, cook for about 15 minutes and add some extra salt if necessary.

5. Do not use more tomatoes then required as the dish gets sour. Maybe that's why we like to add a bit of sugar to this dish.

Wild Mushroom Paprikash

Ingredients:

0.5 dl/1.7 oz oil
1 onion, 2 eggs
1 tablespoon sweet paprika
250 gr/8.8 oz wild champignon
250 gr/8.8 oz oyster mushroom
200 gr/7 oz fairy-ring mushrooms
salt, ground black pepper
1 green pepper, 1 tomato
1 tablespoon flour
1.5 dl/5 oz sour cream
500 gr/18 oz flour
4.5 dl/15 oz water

Preparation:

1. Clean and chop the mushrooms into medium size cubes. Heat the oil in a pot, place the finely chopped onion in it, sauté and then pull aside. Sprinkle with sweet paprika, add the mushrooms. Pour some water to cover the mushroom up to half, boil and then add salt and black pepper. Cook over medium heat. When it is half done, add the sliced green pepper and the tomato and cook until done.
2. Before pulling aside, mix the flour and sour cream with some water and add to the mushroom stew. It is ready when boiled again and thickened.
3. Sprinkle the flour in a bowl, add some salt and the eggs. Mix well with water to get dough, form small dumplings and chop them into boiling water.
4. Serve with dumplings; decorate with sour cream, green pepper and tomato.

Layered Green Beans

Ingredients:

100 gr/3.5 oz rice
1 onion
2 cloves of garlic
2 tablespoons oil
500 gr/18 oz ground pork
2 teaspoons sweet paprika
1/4 teaspoon ground black pepper
1 teaspoon marjoram
800 gr/28 oz green beans
2 dl/6.7 oz sour cream

1 egg
1 bunch of parsley
butter
breadcrumbs
salt

Preparation:

1. Boil 2 dl/6.7 oz water, add a bit of salt, and the rice and cook, covered, until the water evaporates. Pull aside, place a double folded kitchen cloth under the lid and let the rice soften in its own steam.

2. Chop the onion and garlic finely and sauté for 1-2 minutes. Add the minced meat and sauté, stirring, for 4-5 minutes. Add one teaspoon each of salt and sweet paprika, black pepper and marjoram. Let it cool down and then mix with the rice.

3. Chop the green beans into 2,5 cm/1" pieces, place in slightly salty boiling water and cook for 8 minutes.

4. Mix the sour cream and the egg, add some salt and the remaining sweet paprika and finely chopped parsley. Butter the inside of a casserole, coat with breadcrumbs. Layer half of the green beans at the bottom. Pour 3 tablespoons sour cream mixture and pile the meat mixture on it. Cover with the other half of the beans.

5. Pour the remaining sour cream mixture and bake in pre-heated oven (180°C/350F; 165°C/330F in air-convector ovens) for 25 minutes.

6. You can melt some cheese on the top. Cut in four pieces.

Pike-perch Baked Whole

Ingredients:

4 pike-perches (400 gr/14 oz each)
salt
1 potato
120 gr/4.2 oz flour
1 teaspoon sweet paprika
1 teaspoon ground black pepper
1 lemon
oil
8 sour cherries

Preparation:

1. Remove the scales of the fish, open the belly with a sharp knife, and remove the innards, the gills and the eyes. Wash the fish in cold water, pat dry, and then make incisions 2-3 cm/1-1.2" apart. Rub with salt inside and outside and put in a refrigerator, covered, for at least 1 hour.

2. Carefully open the mouth wide and wedge a quarter of a potato. Take the head and the tail of the fish, bend it to back and form croissant-shape.

3. Pierce a sharpened skewer through the neck and the tail to secure the shape, tie with a string if necessary. Mix the flour, sweet paprika and black pepper, and coat the fish with the mixture.

4. Pour some oil in a frying pan. Heat it, and when medium hot, place the fish in carefully and fry it, uncovered, for 5-8 minutes on each side.

5. Carefully remove the fish, and place on a paper towel or a napkin to remove all the excess oil. When serving, replace the potato in the mouth with a piece of lemon. Place them on a plate, and decorate with potatoes sautéed on oil with parsley on both sides.

6. Place sour cherries in the eye sockets. Offer the dish with tartar sauce.

300 gr/10.6 oz flat pasta

Preparation:

1. Fillet the carp. Use the head, the removed bones, an onion sliced and some salt to prepare fish stock, boil them in 3-4 dl/10-13 oz water, and cook for 1/2 hour.
2. Cut the fish 4 big or 8 small, even slices, make incisions by 3-4 mm/ 0.2" almost to the skin.
3. Rub with salt, coat with flour and fry for 3-4 minutes on each side in 5 tablespoonfuls of oil. Place on paper towel to remove the excess oil.
4. Cut the bacon into small cubes, and chop the remaining onions finely. Clean the mushrooms, remove the stems from the pepper and the tomato, then chop the vegetables into 1 cm/0.5" cubes.
5. Fry the bacon on the remaining oil and sauté the onions. Add the mushrooms, pepper and tomato, and after a short time add the sweet paprika.
6. To prevent the paprika from burning, add the strained fish stock immediately and cook for 5 minutes. Mix the sour cream with the remaining flour until smooth, ladle a bit of the hot stock in it to thicken the paprika-mushroom ragout. Add some black pepper and salt if needed.
7. Meanwhile cook the pasta in slightly salty water, strain it and mix with the sour cream ragout. Reheat the fish slices and serve them arranged over the ragout.

Carp as in Dorozsma

Ingredients:

1 carp (kb. 1.2 kg/2.6 lb)
2 onions
salt
3 tablespoons flour
7 tablespoons oil
60 gr/2.1 oz smoked bacon
150 gr/5.3 oz champignons
1 green pepper
1 tomato
1 tablespoon sweet paprika
2 dl/6.7 oz sour cream
1/2 teaspoon ground black pepper

Catfish Paprikash

Ingredients:

4 catfish fillets, skin removed (kb. 1 kg/2.2 lb)
1 tablespoon salt
1 big onion
4 tablespoons oil
1 tablespoon sweet paprika
1 green pepper, 1 tomato
1/2 teaspoon hot paprika cream
1 tablespoon flour
1 dl/3.4 oz sour cream and cream each

Preparation:

1. Cut the catfish fillet into 2-3 cm/1" cubes, rub with the half of the salt around and put aside.
2. Chop the onion finely and sauté in a pan on hot oil. Pull aside, sprinkle with sweet paprika and add 5 dl/17 oz water. Add the finely chopped pepper and tomato, paprika cream and the remaining salt to taste.
3. Over medium heat cook for 30-35 minutes, boil for 2 minutes with a bit of flour smoothly mixed with 1 dl/3.4 oz water to thicken. Press through a sieve or beat with a whisk to obtain a creamy broth then reheat over medium-high heat.
4. Add the salted catfish when the broth is boiling and cook for 5-6 minutes (for 8-10 minutes if the skin is on).
5. Add the spices and 1-2 tablespoons of white wine if you like.
4. Add 1/3.4 oz sour cream and cream each to the stew and boil for few seconds. Serve with dumplings or pasta with curded ewe-cheese.
5. Instead of catfish you can use different fish; e.g. a carp, a sturgeon, a pike and perch-pike too.

Serbian Carp

Ingredients:

800 gr/28 oz carp fillet
150 gr/5.3 oz smoked bacon
salt
1 kg/2.2 lb potato
2 onions
4 green peppers, 4 tomatoes
4 tablespoons oil
1 tablespoon sweet paprika
1 teaspoon hot paprika cream
2 dl/6.7 oz sour cream
1 tablespoon flour

Preparation:

1. Cut the fillet into 4 even slices. Place them on a chopping board with skin down, and make incisions every 0.5 cm/0.2" to the skin.

2. Place a thin slice of bacon in each incision. Rub the fish with some salt and put aside.

3. Cook the potatoes in hot, salty water with their skin on, peel them and cut into rings. Clean the onion, and remove the stem from the peppers and tomatoes. Chop the onion finely, and sauté. Chop the peppers and tomatoes into medium size cubes, and add them to the onion and sauté over high heat for 4-5 minutes. Add salt, paprika and cherry paprika paste. Mix the flour and the sour cream until smooth and then add to the ragout. Boil for 2-3 minutes.

4. Arrange the potato in the middle of a casserole, pour the sour cream mixture on it and place the fish slices around. Pre-heat the oven, and bake the fish over high heat (200 °C / 390 F; 180°C/350F in air-convector ovens) for 15-20 minutes.

FOWL DISHES

Chicken Paprikash

Ingredients:

8 big chicken legs
salt
4 onions
6 tablespoons oil (or 150 gr/5.3 oz smoked bacon)
2 tablespoons sweet paprika
3-4 green peppers
4 tomatoes
1 teaspoon hot paprika paste
3 dl/10 oz sour cream
2-3 tablespoons flour

Preparation:

1. Remove the skin of the chicken legs. Cut the legs at the joint. Place them in a bowl and rub with 1 tablespoon salt.
2. Clean the onion, chop finely and sauté over medium heat. Add 1 tablespoon salt and 3-4 dl/10-13 oz water and sauté for 10-15 minutes.
3. When done, add the salted chicken legs and fry the meat until white. Sprinkle with paprika, stir and add 5-6 dl/17-20 oz water. Clean and remove the stem of the peppers and tomatoes, chop them finely and add to the meat. Add the paprika paste too. When boiling, turn the heat a bit down, cover, and cook for 1 hour until tender. Mix the flour and the sour cream until smooth, add to the stew to thicken and boil for 2-3 minutes.
4. Mix the flour, egg, salt and water to get dough and "chop" it in boiling water. Dumplings are the ideal garnish to the Chicken Paprikash.

Chicken Liver with Pepper and Tomato Stew

Ingredients:

500 gr/18 oz chicken liver
2 onions
3-4 green peppers
2-3 tomatoes
4 tablespoons oil
1 teaspoon salt
1/2 teaspoon ground black pepper
1/2 teaspoon marjoram
1 teaspoon sweet paprika
1 hot paprika
1/2 bunch of parsley

Preparation:

1. Cut the liver into slices (into 2 or 3 slices). Chop the onion finely. Remove the stem of the peppers and tomatoes and then remove their skin. Place them on a board and chop into 3 cm/1.2" cubes.
2. Take a big pan, pour some oil in it and heat. Add the onion and sauté over medium heat while stirring for 6-7 minutes.
3. Add the peppers, sauté for 3 minutes, add the liver, sauté 3 minutes again, and then finally add the tomato cubes. Add salt, black pepper, paprika and marjoram to taste. To make it a bit chilly, you can also add some sliced hot paprika. Mix them over heat for 1-2 minutes.
4. Fry over medium heat for 7-8 minutes – until the liver turns tender and the sauce looks like pepper and tomato stew.
5. When serving, sprinkle with finely chopped parsley. Barley goes well with it.

Turkey Roast as in Brassó

Ingredients:

1.2 kg/2.6 lb potato
salt
800 gr/28 oz turkey thigh fillet
100 gr/3.5 oz smoked bacon
2 tablespoons oil
6 cloves of garlic
1 teaspoon tomato paste
1/2 teaspoon ground black pepper

Preparation:

1. Clean the potatoes and cook them with their skin on. Place them in a bowl and let them cool down.
2. Remove the thin skin from the thighs. Wash the meat, cut into 0.8 cm/0.3" wide Julienne stripes crosswise.
3. Cut the bacon into thin slices. Pour oil in a pan, heat and sauté the bacon in it, over medium heat, for 2 minutes until it turns glassy.
4. Add the meat and sauté until it turns white. Add the ground garlic, tomato paste, black pepper and 1 teaspoon salt to taste. Then add 2 dl/6.7 oz water, bring it to a boil and cook over low heat for 45 minutes.
5. Uncover when ready and sauté the mixture for 3-4 minutes.
6. Peel the potatoes, chop into cubes, fry on hot oil until they turn light brown, and mix with the meat and the sauce.

Chicken Thighs with Dried Plums

Ingredients:

4 chicken thighs
salt, pepper
2 x 1.5 dl/5 oz cream
4 almonds
200 gr/7 oz soft dried plum (pit removed)
2 tablespoons oil
700 gr/24.5 oz potato
1 teaspoon ground black
1/2 teaspoon sweet paprika
butter
milk

Preparation:

1. Peel the potatoes and chop them into small cubes. Place the cubes into cold, slightly salty water and bring the water to a boil. The water has to cover the potato completely but do not let the foam boil over. Cook until tender (depends on the type how much time it requires) and to prevent from being overcooked check with a fork occasionally. Strain and mash the cooked potatoes with hot milk and a little butter or baking margarine. You can add some sour cream then salt to it.
2. Wash and dry the chicken thighs. Rub them all around with salt and black pepper.
3. Place the cleaned almonds into the middle of the dried plums then push them under the skin of the chicken thighs.
4. Place them in a casserole, arrange nicely and add some oil (you can add a bit of water too). Arrange the rest of the plums around the meat, cover the casserole with foil and bake over medium heat (180°C/350F; 165°C/330F in air convector ovens) for 1 hour.
5. For the last 10 minutes remove the foil to let the meat gain a nice reddish color. Pour the cooking cream on the meat and bake for additional 2-3 minutes.
6. Serve with mashed potatoes.

Classic Goose Roast

1 kg/2.2 lb red (or white) cabbage
1 tablespoon vinegar
50 gr/1.8 oz butter

Preparation:

1. Clean the meat, salt and rub them around with marjoram, and then place in a rimmed casserole. Add 2 dl/6.7 oz water, cover with foil and bake over low heat (170°C/340F; 155°C/310F in air-convector ovens) for two hours.
2. Turn the meat several times, basting with the juice every time, and uncover when half done. The meat will be tender if you bake it slowly.
3. To prepare the stewed cabbage remove the strunk of the cabbage then slice cabbage into thin stripes. Thinly slice the onion.
4. Pour the oil in a pot and sauté the sugar for 2-3 minutes until it turns light brown. Add the onion first and then the cabbage. Add the salt to it, spice with caraway seeds and black pepper. Bring it to a boil, cook covered, over low heat for 25 minutes untiltender (stir once or twice). Add the vinegar when the cabbage is done.
5. Cook the potatoes in their skin in lightly salty water and then strain. Let them cool down then peel and grate using apple-shredder.
6. Clean the onion, chop finely, place in a pot and sauté on melted butter, stirring continuously, for 2-3 minutes. Add the potatoes, taste with salt, black pepper and a bit of marjoram and sauté, stirring for additional 4-5 minutes, until it turns golden. Press into a ladle or a small bowl and place on the plate.
7. Arrange the meat and the cabbage around it.

Ingredients:

4 goose thighs (400 gr/14 oz each)
salt
marjoram
1.2 kg/2.6 lb potato
2.5 onions
4 tablespoons oil
2 tablespoons sugar
 ground caraway seeds
 ground black pepper

Pullet Breast Filled with Quail's Eggs and Wild Mushrooms

Ingredients:

500 gr/18 oz chicken breast fillet
80 gr/2.8 oz wild mushroom mixture
2 spring onions, 1/2 bunch of wild garlic
2 tablespoons oil
1 bunch of parsley
salt, ground black and white pepper
4 hard boiled quail eggs, 3 eggs
3 tablespoons breadcrumbs
250 gr/9 oz buckwheat
1 tablespoon soy oil, 20 gr/0.7 oz butter
3-4 leaves pre-cooked savoy cabbage
lovage, buttermilk, starch

Preparation:

1. Pierce the chicken breasts with a sharp knife to form pockets. Chop the mushroom, onion and parsley finely and chop the quail eggs into small cubes. Pour oil in a pan, heat it and add the onion. Sauté it on hot oil, add the mushrooms, and spice with salt, black pepper and parsley. Add the quail eggs and breadcrumbs. Push the mixture into the pockets, wrap them in buttered foil and bake in pre-heated oven over 180°C/350F (165°C/330F in air-convector ovens) for 30 minutes.
2. Mix the buckwheat cooked in salty water with some salt, soy oil, black pepper, finely chopped wild garlic, egg yolks, beaten egg whites and breadcrumbs. Lightly butter a narrow roasting pan, place the cabbage leaves in it, and then place the buckwheat mixture on the leaves. Place the narrow roasting pan in a baking dish filled with water and then put in a pre-heated oven. Slowly bake/steam for 20-25 minutes until it is done.
3. Melt the butter in a pan, add the finely chopped lovage and sauté a bit and then add some white wine and about 1 dl/3.4 oz water to it. Bring it to a boil and thicken using the buttermilk mixed with starch.
4. Remove the foil, cut the meat askew into three parts, and place them on the plates. Slice the buckwheat soufflé into thin pieces, place next to the meat and pour the sauce on the plates.
5. Serve with vegetables steamed in butter.

PORK DISHES

Hungarian Pork Fillet

Ingredients:

700 gr/25 oz pork fillet
salt
ground black pepper
1 kg potato
10 tablespoons pepper and tomato stew
1/2 bunch of parsley
oil

Preparation:

1. Remove the thin skin from the meat, cut into 12 round pieces, flatten a bit and then add salt and maybe a touch of black pepper.
2. Peel the potatoes, and chop into 0.3 cm/0.1" rings. Dry them and fry on hot oil (or in deep-fryer) until they turn golden. Place them on paper towel to remove the excess oil.
3. Meanwhile place the meat slices in a pan, fry on little oil for 3 minutes on each side, then place on paper towel to remove the excess oil. Salt the potatoes, mix with the pepper and tomato stew thoroughly and place on plates.
4. Place the fried meat on the potato and pepper and tomato stew and decorate with chopped parsley.
5. You can prepare loin or sirloin slices in the same way.

Stuffed Marrow with Cream and Dill Sauce

Ingredients:

500 gr/18 oz minced pork
1 egg, 2 rolls
2-3 spring onions
1 teaspoon salt
1/2 teaspoon ground black pepper
1 big bunch of dill
2 pcs. ½ kg tender marrows

1 tablespoon spice mixture or 2 bouillon cubes
1.5 dl/ 5 oz sour cream
2 dl/6.7 oz cream
2 tablespoons flour
juice from 1/2 lemon

Preparation:

1. Soak the rolls in cold water and squeeze. Mix them with the minced meat and the egg.
2. Chop the green onion finely, add to the meat mixture, and add some salt, black pepper and 1 tablespoon chopped dill. Wash the marrows and cut the ends. Cut them into half lengthwise, and remove the soft inside and seeds.
3. Fill the cavity with the meat mixture, and then place the marrows into a pot. Pour about 6 dl/20 oz water in the pot. Bring it to a boil over high heat and cook, covered, for 30-35 minutes.
4. Remove the stuffed marrows from the pot. Mix the sour cream, cooking cream and flour in a bowl until smooth and add a bit of the cooking water to it. Then pour the smooth mixture into the pot, bring it to a boil and cook, stirring, for 2-3 minutes until it thickens. Taste it, add some salt if needed, and then spice with the remaining dill and a few drops of lemon juice.
5. Place a half stuffed marrow on each plate and serve with dill sauce.

Pork Chops Serbian Style

<u>Ingredients:</u>

8 slices of (80 gr/3 oz each) pork chops
8 slices of (120 gr/4.2 oz) smoked bacon
1.2 kg/2.6 lb potato, 2 onions
300 gr/10.5 oz champignons
4-4 green peppers and tomatoes
4 tablespoons oil, 2 dl/6.7 oz sour cream
1 tablespoon sweet paprika, salt
1 teaspoon hot paprika paste

<u>Preparation:</u>

1. Flatten the pork chops, make incisions at the ends and rub thoroughly with salt. Roll each slice of bacon around a slice of meat.
2. Cook the potatoes in salty water in their skin on. Strain and let them cool down, peel and chop into 0.5 cm/0.2" thick rings. Clean the onions, mushroom, peppers and tomatoes and remove the stems.
3. Chop the onion finely and sauté on hot oil for 4-5 minutes until it turns yellow. Add the mushroom and sauté for another 4-5 minutes, stirring, in order to prevent it from burning.
4. Chop the peppers and tomatoes into 2.5 cm/1" cubes; add them to the onion mushroom mixture and sauté together for 6 minutes. Flavor it with 1 teaspoon salt and paprika paste. Add the sour cream, bring it to a boil and cook for 2-3 minutes until thickens.
5. Arrange the potatoes in a casserole nicely and pour the mushroom-sour cream "stew" on. Place the pork chops rolled in bacon on top and bake, in pre-heated oven, over medium heat (180°C/350F; 165°C/330F in air-convector ovens) for about 20 minutes.

Pork Ribs as in Bakony the way Puskas Liked It

Ingredients:

10 pcs. (80 gr/3 oz each) pork ribs
100 gr/3.5 oz lard
60 gr/2 oz smoked bacon
150 gr/5.3 oz onion
400 gr/14 oz mushroom
2 dl/6.7 oz sour cream
1 dl/3.4 oz cream
3 green peppers
1 tomato
50 gr/1.8 oz flour
1 clove of garlic
sweet paprika, salt
ground caraway seeds

Preparation:

1. Flatten the pork ribs and rub them thoroughly with salt. Coat with flour and fry on hot lard until they turn white, and then place them in a pot. Chop the onion finely, sauté in the remaining lard, and add some sweet paprika and water to it.
2. Chop the cleaned and washed mushrooms, green peppers and tomato into cubes and add them to the onion. Add the garlic and the caraway seeds to taste. Chop the bacon into small cubes, fry the cubes a bit in a frying pan and add to the mushrooms. Mix them, cover, and cook over medium heat until half-done. Add the half-done ribs to it, shake the pot, and cook, covered, until tender.
3. Mix the sour cream and the cream with a bit of flour until smooth, add the mixture to the meat and boil. Serve with dumplings or rice.

Transylvanian Pork Stew

Ingredients:

800 gr/28 oz pork, chopped into large cubes
100 gr/3.5 oz smoked meaty bacon
1 onion, 2 cloves of garlic
1 tablespoon tomato paste
2 dl/6.7 oz dry white wine
3 celery leaves
salt, ground black pepper

Preparation:

1. Cut the pork cubes into even slices, wash and then dry them. Slice the bacon into strips. Pour oil in a frying pan, place the bacon and fry. Add the cleaned and finely chopped onion and the ground garlic.

2. Sauté a bit together, and then add the prepared meat and continue sautéing until the meat turns white. Add some salt, black pepper, and tomato paste to taste. Pour the white wine and 1 dl/3.4 oz water to it.

3. Mix them, bring to a boil then cover and cook over medium heat until tender. From time to time replace the evaporated sauce by adding some water. Before removing from the heat add the cleaned and finely chopped celery leaves and cook for 1-2 minutes. Serve hot.

4. Serve with rice, potato or corn porridge.

Gipsy Roast

Ingredients:

4 slices (140 gr/5 oz each) of de-boned pork
chop
salt
ground black pepper
2 tablespoons flour
80 gr/2.8 oz smoked bacon
1 onion
80 gr/2.8 oz smoked sausage
1 green pepper, 1 tomato
4 eggs
6 tablespoons oil
fried potato rings
pickles

Preparation:

1. Flatten the pork chop, remove or slit in the thin skin. Slightly rub them with salt and coat with flour.
2. Chop the bacon into 0.5 cm/0.2" cubes and chop the onion finely. Slice the sausage into thin rings. Chop the pepper and the tomato into 1-1.5 cm/0.4-0.6" cubes. Put the eggs in a bowl, add a touch of salt and beat with a fork.
3. Put 2 tablespoons of oil in a frying pan, heat and add the bacon. Fry until crisp, stirring occasionally. Add the onion and sauté it, stirring. Add the sausage and the peppers, sauté them together for a few minutes. Add the tomato, sauté together a bit then at last add the beaten eggs. Fry stirring, until the eggs are almost done.
4. Heat the rest of the oil in another frying pan, and place the meat slices coated in flour in it. Fry them for 2-3 minutes on each side until they gain a nice reddish color.
5. Serving: place some sliced and fried potatoes in the middle of 4 wooden plates. Place the meat on the potatoes then put the scrambled eggs, bacon, sausage and vegetable stew mixture on top. Arrange different dripped pickles around it.

1/4 teaspoon ground white pepper
salt
caper
1 dl/3.4 oz white wine
2 carrots
1 parsnip
1 teaspoon mustard
a dash of sugar
1/2 lemon
1.5 dl/5 oz sour cream

Preparation:

1. Cut the steak across into 4 even slices, flatten the slices and rub around with a dash of salt and then coat with flour. Pour oil in a pan, heat, place the steak in and pre-fry for 2 minutes.
2. In the remaining oil sauté the finely chopped onion. Add the steak, pour on half of the wine and add the ground pepper and bay leaf to taste. Add a little water and cook it, covered, until tender.
3. Meanwhile chop the parsley finely. Wash and clean the carrots and the parsnip and chop them into thin slices.
4. Add them to the almost tender meat, add the mustard, sugar and lemon juice. You can also add a few capers. Pour a bit of water and steam, covered, over low heat for 15 minutes.
5. When done the vegetables should be a bit crunchy.
6. Mix the sour cream with the remaining flour (about 1 tablespoon) and the remaining wine, use it to thicken the vegetable sauce of the steak.
7. Add some salt and serve with spaghetti.

Braised Steak a la Esterhazy

Ingredients:

600 gr/21 oz de-boned sirloin steak
2 tablespoons flour
4 tablespoons oil
1 onion
1 whole bay leaf
1/2 bunch of parsley

Stew with Black Pepper

Ingredients:

600 gr/21 oz de-boned chuck
1 onion, 3 cloves of garlic
5 tablespoons oil
1 tablespoon flour, 1 teaspoon salt
1/2 teaspoon ground black pepper
0.5 dl/1.7 oz dry white wine
1 teaspoon tomato paste

Preparation:

1. Cut the meat across into 0.5 cm/0.2" thick pieces and then slice them into small pieces. Wash and clean the onion, cut into half and then slice into thin pieces.

2. Pour oil in a pan. Heat a bit and sauté the onion on it. Add the meat and fry, stirring until the meat turns white at the ends. Add some salt, black pepper and ground garlic to taste and pour 2 dl/6.7 oz water under it. Bring it to a boil and cook, covered, over low heat for 1.5 hours until very tender. Stir regularly and replace the evaporated juices with a bit of water – you need about 2 dl/6.7 oz water every 20 minutes.

3. Add the wine and the tomato paste when almost done. It is very important to steam it in little water to prevent the meal from having boiled meat taste. The sauce should look like a stew.

4. Serve with crushed boiled potatoes mixed with sautéed onions.

5. To make it juicier mix 1 tablespoon flour with 1.5 dl/5 oz water until smooth. Add to the dish when ready and boil for 1-2 minutes.

Braised Beef in Piquant Brown Sauce

Ingredients:

800 gr/28 oz beef chops or legs
1 onion
300 gr/10.5 oz carrots and parsnips together
2 dl/6.7 oz dry white wine
5 tablespoons oil
1 tablespoon sugar
ground black pepper, salt
2 bay leaves
1 teaspoon mustard
1 lemon
1 tablespoon flour

2 dl/6.7 oz sour cream

Preparation:

1. Add 1 teaspoon salt to 1 1/34 oz water and bring it to a boil. Add the finely chopped onion and half of the vegetables. Cook for 5 minutes then add the wine. Let it cool. Pour in a glass or porcelain dish. Add the meat cutting the legs into 4 cm/1.5" cubes but leave the chops in one piece. Add some water to cover completely. Covered, put in a refrigerator for 2-3 days, turning the meat occasionally.

2. Before cooking pat the meat dry, place in a pan and fry on oil until it turns white. Set aside. Melt the sugar in the remaining oil until silky brown and add the sliced onion and chopped vegetables. Add the salt, bay leaves and black pepper to taste and continue frying. 2-3 minutes later pour on the marinade with the vegetables, add the mustard and lemon juice. Bring to a boil.

3. Add the meat and steam, covered, for 1.5 hours until tender. Replace the evaporating water.

4. When ready, slice the meat perpendicular to the grain. Let the marinade cool, remove the bay leaves, puree it with a mixer and bring to a boil again. Mix the sour cream with the flour and a bit of sauce until smooth and add to the puree to thicken.

5. Pour it over the meat when serving. It goes well with bread dumplings or croquettes.

Sirloin Scones with Roquefort

Ingredients:

600 gr/21 oz sirloin
ground black pepper
mustard
salt
150 gr/5.3 oz Roquefort cheese
1/4 teaspoon sweet paprika
2 tomatoes
4 big but thin slices of edam cheese
oil

Preparation:

1. Remove the thin skin (if there is any) from the sirloin. Rub the meat with a bit of black pepper and spread with mustard. Oil a piece of foil and pack the meat in it. Place in refrigerator and leave there for 3-4 days.

2. After removing from the refrigerator cut the meat into 4 even slices and flatten a bit. Add some salt, black pepper, spread mustard on. Fry on little oil over very high heat for 2 minutes on each side. Let the slices drip and then place them in a baking dish. Grate the Roquefort, add sweet paprika to it and pile over the meat. Place tomato rings on top and cover the whole meal with cheese slices.

3. Place in a grill for 4-5 minutes while it gets hot and the cheese melts on it nicely.

Veal Ragout – Paprikash

Ingredients:

700 gr/24.7 oz de-boned veal shoulder or leg
1 onion
4 tablespoons oil
1 teaspoon sweet paprika
1-1 green pepper and tomato
2 cloves of garlic
1/4 teaspoon ground caraway seeds
1 teaspoon salt
1/2 teaspoon hot paprika paste
1.5 dl/5 oz sour cream
1 teaspoon flour

Preparation:

1. Remove the ligaments and the thin skin from the meat. Chop it into 2 cm/0.8" cubes. Chop the onion finely.

2. Heat the oil in a pot. Place the onion in the pot and sauté, over low heat, stirring. Add the meat and continue frying until it turns white. Remove from the heat and add sweet paprika. Add the chopped pepper and tomato, then the crushed garlic, caraway seeds, salt and paprika paste to favor. Pour 1.5 dl/5 oz water over it and steam, covered, for about 1.5 hours until tender. Replace the evaporated water only by small amounts, so that the meat stews rather than cooks. When done it should have a thick, creamy sauce.

3. This is the veal ragout. To prepare the "paprikash", thicken it with sour cream sauce. Mix the sour cream and flour with a bit of cold water until smooth, add it to the ragout, bring it to a boil and cook for 2-3 minutes stirring. If it is too thick, add a bit more water or cooking cream.

4. Serve with home made dumplings.

Pheasant Breast Roast Filled with Dried Plums served with Pear in Red Wine

Ingredients:

4 pears, 2 pheasant breasts
5 dl/17 oz red wine
2 tablespoons sugar, salt
150 gr/5.3 oz pitted soft dried plum
10 corianders, 1 bay leaf
20 gr/0.7 oz butter, 2 tablespoons oil
1 tablespoon breadcrumbs
4 thin slices of bacon, 1 egg

Preparation:

1. Peel the pears but do not remove the stem. Cut a bit off from the bottom. Remove the core from the bottom side; this way the pear can stand separately on the plate, and does not fall over.

2. Pour the red wine in a pan. Boil with some sugar, place the pears in it and steam together for 6-8 minutes until half done.

3. Place the dried plums in a pan, ladle 1 dl/3.4 oz wine juice from the pear, and taste with coriander and bay leaf. Boil and cook over high heat until the liquid evaporates. Let it cool down, remove the spices, and then add butter, egg and breadcrumbs and mix.

4. Cut the pheasant breasts in half to make 4 fillets. Pierce them alongside in the middle and fill with plum mixture.

5. Add a bit of salt, roll the fillets in bacon slices and pre-fry them in iron pan on hot oil. When done, place in pre-heated oven and bake, over medium heat (160°C/360 F; 150°C/300 F in air-convector ovens), for 12 minutes. Serve with steamed rice and pear in hot wine. Cumberland sauce goes well with it, too.

Venison Roast

Ingredients:

800 gr/28 oz venison saddle
1 tablespoon mustard
1/2 teaspoon ground black pepper
salt, oil
120 gr/4.2 oz smoked bacon

Preparation:

1. Remove the thin white skin from the venison saddle and rub thoroughly with the mixture of mustard and black pepper. Place it tightly in a pan and pour enough oil over it to cover the meat. Cover with a lid or cloth and leave in refrigerator for 2-3 days. Turn it occasionally.
2. After removing from the refrigerator let it drip, place on a cutting board and make lengthwise (parallel with the fibers) incisions every 0.5 cm/0.2". Place smoked bacon slices into the incisions then add salt.
3. Put 6-8 tablespoons of the oil used for marinating into a pan, heat and sauté the venison around. Place the venison in a baking dish, pour the hot oil over it, and put in a pre-heated oven (200°C/390 F, 180°C/350 F in air-convector ovens).
4. You can bake it rare, medium or tender. To make it rare, the meat should be done only on the outside, the inside is pink, and the very middle is raw. This requires about 17-20 minutes baking. The medium version requires about 20-23 minutes baking and not only the skin is done but the inside as well, one centimeter deep, the middle is pink but no blood in it. The well-done version requires 5-6 more minutes baking.
5. Place on a plate when ready. Serve with vegetables steamed on butter and offer some brown sauce with it.
6. Slice the roast at the table when serving. First remove the meat from the bone in one piece then slice it.

Leg of Hare in Piquant Sauce with Noodles flavored with Onion

Ingredients:

4 legs of hare (kb. 1.6 kg/3.5 lb)
150 gr/5.3 oz smoked bacon
ground black pepper, salt
12 tablespoons oil
2carrots, 2 parsleys, 1/2 celery
5 onions, 1 clove of garlic
2 bay leaves, thyme
2 tablespoons flour, 3 dl/10 oz sour cream
1 l/34 oz strained bouillon
2 dl/6.5 oz white wine, juice of 1/2 lemon
1 tablespoon sugar
1 tablespoon mustard
1 small bottle of (70 gr/3.5 oz) anchovy rings
500 gr/18 oz potato dumplings (can be frozen!)

Preparation:

1. Remove the thin white skin from the meat. Cut the bacon into 0.5 cm/0.2" slices and lard the meat with it. Rub with salt and black pepper. Pour some oil in a pan, heat and sauté the meat.
2. Chop all the vegetables and add them to the meat. Add the bay leaves and thyme to taste, sauté for 4-5 minutes and sprinkle with the flour. Sauté for 1-2 minutes stirring. Then pour the bouillon and wine over it, bring to a boil over high heat and cook, over low heat, covered, for 1.5 hours until tender.
3. When ready remove the tender meat from the pan. Add sugar, lemon and mustard to the sauce to give a piquant flavor. Add the sour cream and add half of the anchovy rings (4 small fillets). Boil for 1-2 minutes and mash. When serving, pour over the legs.
4. Serve with noodles flavored with onion. First cook the noodles. Chop the onion into rings, separate the rings and sauté them over medium heat until they turn golden. Salt them a bit and add to the noodles.

Deer Ragout a la Hunter

Ingredients:

600 gr/21 oz de-boned deer leg or shoulder
ground thyme, 4 tablespoons oil
ground black pepper, salt
200 gr/7 oz oyster mushroom
4 dl/13.5 oz brown sauce
150 gr/5.3 oz canned tangerines
50 gr/1.8 oz almonds cut into thin slices

Preparation:

1. Chop the meat into 2 cm/0.8" cubes and rub with thyme and black pepper. Add 4 tablespoons oil and leave, covered, in a refrigerator for 2 days.
2. Remove from the refrigerator and place it in a pan. Fry on oil until it turns white and add some salt. Pour a bit of water over and steam, covered, for 1.5 hours until tender. Replace the evaporating water continuously.
3. Clean the mushrooms, chop them into 2 cm/0.8" cubes and add to the meat. Fry for 5 minutes uncovered then add the brown sauce and the tangerines. Boil for 2 minutes and finally add the almonds.
4. Serve with croquettes.

Gundel Pancake

Ingredients:

4.5 dl/15 oz milk, 1 dl/3.4 oz cream
250 gr/8.8 oz confectioner's sugar
1 pack vanilla sugar
200 gr/7 oz ground walnuts
50 gr/1.8 oz raisins
1/2 lemon rind
1 tablespoon + 0.3 dl/1 oz rum
ground cinnamon
1 dl/3.4 oz cream, whipped
12 pancakes, 2 egg yolks
20 gr/0.8 oz butter, 1 teaspoon flour
150 gr/5 oz dark chocolate

Preparation:

1. Boil the milk with the confectioner's sugar and add the walnuts. Pull aside, add the raisins and mix. Then add a few drops of rum, lemon rind and cinnamon to give nice flavor. Let cool then add the whipped cream to loosen.

2. Fill the pancakes with this soft walnut cream. Fold them into quarters and arrange them next to each other in a buttered casserole.

3. Mix the sugar, egg yolks, 1 dl/3.4 oz milk and flour until smooth. Boil the remaining milk with the vanilla sugar, the cream and the broken chocolate until the chocolate dissolves. Add the flour mixture and boil stirring with a whisk for 3 minutes – until it thickens into a sauce. Pull aside and then add the remaining rum.

4. Pour the sauce on the pancakes. Heat them with the sauce on in medium hot oven for a few minutes.

Floating Islands

Ingredients:

4 eggs
120 gr/4.2 oz sugar
1 l/34 oz milk
half vanillin rod or 1-2 packs of vanilla sugar
1 teaspoon vanilla pudding powder

Preparation:

1. Separate the yolks from the egg whites. Beat the egg whites for a few minutes. Add the sugar and whip until very stiff peaks form. Put aside 1 dl/3.4 oz milk. Put the remaining milk with the rest of the sugar and the vanillin rod split into half and cleaned/vanilla sugar in a pan and bring to a boil.

2. With a tablespoon dripped in milk drop a few spoonfuls of beaten egg whites on the top of the boiling milk. Not too many at a time – leave some room for them to grow. Boil them for half a minute, turn and leave in the milk for another half a minute. Cut one to check if it is done. When done, drip and place them on a dish.

3. Mix the egg yolks, cold milk put aside and pudding powder with a whisk until smooth. Continue beating, pour this egg mixture into the hot milk and cook (without boiling) until thickens a bit.

4. Serve cold, in a glass dish with the egg white dumplings on top.

Poppy Seed Dough

Ingredients:

400 gr/14 oz flour
20 gr/0.7 oz yeast
a dash of salt, 1/2 teaspoon sugar
100 gr/3.5 oz confectioner's sugar
8 dl/27 oz milk, 1.5 dl/5 oz water
20 gr/0.7 oz butter, 50 gr/1.8 oz melted butter
150 gr/5.3 oz ground poppy seed

Preparation:

1. Sieve the flour in a dish and mix thoroughly with yeast. Dissolve the salt and sugar in luke-warm milk stirring with a teaspoon. Pour it over the flour and start kneading. Meanwhile add the melted (but – very important! – not warm) butter and knead it for about 6-8 minutes. We should get a medium hard dough similar to pizza dough which can be easily separated from the side of the dish. Immediately take it into halves, form nice small buns and leave them in warm place for 15 minutes.

2. Form 3.5 cm/1.4" wide, 40 cm/16" long rods from the buns. Place them in a baking dish, let rise for 1 hour in a warm place. Smear with wet brush and place them in pre-heated oven. Bake over relatively high heat (200°C/390F; 180°C/350F in air-convector ovens) for 20-22 minutes. Remove from the oven, wet them a bit and let them cool.

3. Cut them into 1 cm/0.5" rings and soak the rings in small portions in hot milk. When soaked a bit, remove them carefully with a straining ladle. Drip them and arrange the rings in a small buttered baking dish or casserole.

4. Mix the poppy seed and the sugar. Sprinkle the rings with it, put another layer on and sprinkle again with the poppy seed and sugar. Bake over high heat (200°C/390F; 180°C/350F in air-convector ovens) for 10-12 minutes.

500 gr/18 oz pitted soft dried plum
1 pack (8 pieces) strudel pastry
200 gr/7 oz ground walnuts
100 gr/3.5 oz melted butter
8 teaspoons honey
1 teaspoon ground cinnamon
butter
1 egg

for the chocolate coating:

2 tablespoons milk
20 gr/0.7 oz dark cocoa powder
80 gr/3 oz butter or baking margarine
80 gr/3 oz sugar
2 tablespoons starch

Preparation:

1. Chop the plums into quarters. Place 4 strudel pastries on a wet kitchen cloth. Sprinkle with walnuts. Then arrange the plums on it and pour the melted butter or margarine and honey over it.
2. Sprinkle with cinnamon then roll them up. Place the rolls in a lined or buttered baking dish. Spread the beaten eggs on top of the rolls.
3. Bake in oven over medium heat (180°C/350F; 165°C/330F in air-convector ovens) for twenty-five minutes.
4. Cook the ingredients of the chocolate coating together over low heat. Let cool and spread it on the cold strudels. Slice the rolls only when the chocolate coating has hardened.

Strudel Filled with Dried Plums and Walnut in Chocolate Coating

Ingredients:

CONTENT

ISBN 978 963 87076 5 9

☎: + 36-30-224-3223

© Published in Hungary